The Wee Scottish Recipe Book

by Margaret Mochrie

Table of Contents

1. Welcome to Scotland!

Thank you so much for picking up this book and wanting to discover the joys of Scottish cooking. There is plethora of cookbooks out there showing thousands of recipes from all around the world, but sometimes the best things are right on your doorstep. That is why I, a proud Scot, have put together this collection of Scottish recipes that I know represent traditional Scottish cooking at its best.
I hope you enjoy these recipes and you enjoy eating them as much as I have over the years.

- Margaret Mochrie

2. East Coast Cullen Skink

Cullen Skink is a traditional, thick and filling soup made from smoked haddock, potatoes and onions. It originates from the North east of Scotland, a part of the country where the fishing industry thrives. You will now find this dish served up all over the country and it pleases my heart when I see it on the menu of the poshest or humblest eatery in town.

Ingredients:

4 fillets of smoked haddock (cut into wee pieces)
Half a wee onion (diced)
3 pints of whole milk
4 tablespoons of single cream
1 oz butter
2 teaspoons cornflour (mixed with a tablespoon of milk)
4 medium potatoes (part boiled and diced)

Method:

Melt the butter in a large saucepan, add the onion and smoked haddock and simmer for 2 minutes.

Add the part boiled potatoes and milk, and bring to the boil.

Add the cornflour mixed with a tablespoon of milk.

Cook for 2 minutes and then add the cream prior to serving.

This is delicious when served with fresh buttered brown bread.

3. Cock-a-Leekie Soup

This is often called 'Scotland's National Soup' and it has been made in Scotland for years.The name is self explanatory; Chicken (Cock) and Leek (Leekie) soup, which raises a snigger to many a young schoolboy.

The addition of prunes is thought to come from a time when only wild birds were available to the normal folk and they were added to boost the soups nutritional value.

Nowadays cooked rice is sometimes added to give the soup more weight but I prefer it the traditional way, unadulterated.

Ingredients:

6 chicken drumsticks or 3 whole chicken legs
700ml-1 litre of water
1 onion finely chopped
2 leeks sliced
2 carrots chopped
12 prunes chopped
2 sprigs thyme
1 bay leaf
Salt and pepper

Method:

Preheat your oven to 200c / 400f / gas mark 6. Roast the chicken pieces for around 30 minutes then place in a heavy bottomed pot along with the cooked chicken juices.

Add water until the chicken pieces are just covered then bring to the boil and simmer for 1 hour to create a stock.

Add in the vegetables, prunes, herbs, a good grinding of pepper and half a teaspoon of salt. Cook the vegetables for about 20 minutes until tender. Remove the chicken, take the meat from the bones and stir back into soup.

Discard the bones and the herbs, season with salt and pepper and serve straight away with some delicious crusty bread.

Try this soup the day after you make it, the flavours combine and, in my opinion, taste better.

4. Mother's Scotch Broth

This traditional filling soup made of lamb, root vegetables and barley was a staple lunchtime meal in my household when growing up as was a great way of using leftovers. It wasn't always lamb that was used, beef, ham or even chicken was added, depending on what mother had in the fridge, but it was when she used lamb that it tasted best. I still often make this recipe, especially in the cold winter months.

Ingredients:
1lb mutton or neck of lamb
3 pints of water
1oz pearl barley and 2oz dried peas, soaked overnight
1 large carrot sliced,
1 large onion diced,
1 small leek sliced,
1 small diced turnip
4oz shredded cabbage
1 level tablespoon of chopped parsley

Method:
Trim any excess fat from the mutton and put in a large pan with the water, pearl barley, peas and seasoning.

Bring to the boil and simmer for an hour.

Add the carrot, onion, leek and turnip, return to the boil and simmer for another 30 minutes or until the vegetables are just cooked.

Add the cabbage and cook for another 15 minutes.

Remove the mutton from the pot and trim off the meat into small pieces and return it to the pot, discarding the bones.

Skim off any fat, season to taste and garnish with a few pinches of parsley.

5. Potted Meat

'Potting' meat is a traditional way of preserving meat. Chopped meat would be set in butter or, as in this case, a gelatinous brine made from the meat juices and bone marrow. This is a delicious to serve as a starter like a terrine or sliced in a sandwich.

Ingredients:

3 lbs beef shank with bone & marrow
1 veal knuckle bone
1 bay leaf
6 peppercorns

Method:

Cover the beef shank and veal knuckle with cold water and add the bay leaf and peppercorns then bring to a boil.

Cover and simmer gently for 3 hours.

When done drain the liquid (stock) into a separate pan.

Remove the bones and gristle from the meat.

Chop the meat up fine and return to stock add salt & pepper to taste.

Bring everything to a boil again to blend then remove pan from heat and let contents cool.

When cool (not cold) empty mixture into a terrine mold and chill in the fridge.

When set take slice and serve as a starter with a sweet fruit chutney or serve in a sandwich with a mild mustard.

6. Clapshot with Bacon

Clapshot is a traditional potato dish, often served with grilled red meats, which originated on the Orkney Isles to the north of Scotland's mainland. It does not traditionally have bacon included but I feel that this addition adds a delicious flavour and texture to the dish.

Ingredients:

600g potatoes, peeled and quartered
300g turnips, peeled and cut into chunks
45g butter
60ml milk
8 bacon rashers, cooked until crisp and crumbled
1/4 tsp freshly-grated nutmeg
salt and freshly-ground black pepper, to taste.

Method:

Add the potatoes and turnip to a large pan, cover with lightly-salted water and bring to a boil.

Continue cooking until they are tender (about 20 minutes).

Drain the vegetables in a colander then return to the pan and mash until smooth.

Add the butter and milk to the potatoes then mash in and beat until smooth and fluffy.

Stir-in the crumbled bacon and season with the nutmeg, salt and black pepper.

Serve as a side dish for roasted or grilled meats or meat pies.

7. Traditional Stovies

Stovies is a particularly brilliant dish that the Scots love to eat as the perfect comfort food, especially while watching their rugby team win or lose at the local pub. Today there are many variations of this recipe. Basic recipes are a mix of mash potatoes, onions and either sliced sausage, bacon or corned beef, but this recipe is the best and most authentic. Enjoy over the winter months.

Ingredients:

4 oz cold, diced lamb
1½ lb potatoes, peeled and sliced.
1 large onion, very thinly sliced.
1 level tablespoon (from bacon is best). If dripping is not available, cooking oil will do
Stock or water
Salt and pepper for seasoning
Chopped parsley or chives

Method:

Melt the dripping in a large pan (preferably with a tight fitting lid), add a layer of sliced potatoes, then a layer of onion and next a layer of meat.

Add enough stock or water to cover (though some prefer their stovies dry, in which case add only 2-3 tablespoons). Then repeat the layers once again and season the dish thoroughly with salt and pepper.

Cover and cook over a low to moderate heat (shaking the pan occasionally) for about 30 minutes or until the potatoes are tender and the liquid is absorbed.

Serve with a sprinkling of chopped parsley or chives.

8. Haggis From Scratch

No Scottish cookbook would be complete without a mention, or indeed, a recipe for Haggis. To be honest very few Scots actually make haggis from scratch. The ingredients are ridiculously cheap, so ready made haggis is also cheap, but we love it and we buy it a lot. It comes in sheep's stomach, it comes in sausage skin or it comes in a tin. On burns night it is celebrated as a god like entity, addressed with a poem by the Scottish Bard, Robert Burns:

Tae a Haggis
Fair fa' your honest, sonsie face,
Great chieftain o the puddin'-race!
Aboon them a' ye tak your place,
Painch, tripe, or thairm:
Weel are ye worthy o' a grace
As lang's my arm.

Ingredients:

1 sheep's stomach, cleaned and thoroughly, scalded, turned inside out and soaked overnight in cold salted water
Heart, liver and lungs of one lamb
450g/1lb beef or lamb trimmings
2 onions, finely chopped
225g/8oz oatmeal
1 tbsp salt
1 tsp ground black pepper
1 tsp mace
1 tsp nutmeg
water, enough to cook the haggis
stock from lungs and trimmings

Method:

Wash the lungs, heart and liver. Place in large pan of cold water with the meat trimmings and bring to the boil. Cook for about 2 hours.

When cooked, strain off the stock and set the stock aside.

Mince the lungs, heart and trimmings.

Put the minced mixture in a bowl and add the finely chopped onions, oatmeal and seasoning. Mix well and add enough stock to moisten the mixture. It should have a soft crumbly consistency.

Spoon the mixture into the sheep's stomach, so it's just over half full.

Sew up the stomach with strong thread and prick a couple of times so it doesn't explode while cooking.

Put the haggis in a pan of boiling water (enough to cover it) and cook for 3 hours without a lid.

Keep adding more water to keep it covered.

To serve, cut open the haggis and spoon out the filling. Serve with neeps (mashed swede or turnip) and tatties (mashed potatoes).

9. Hotch Potch

This is a traditional Scottish soup which should be extremely thick and served with crusty bread and butter. It is a meal in itself really. Having this as a child it would fill me up all day, in fact this was sometimes served at breakfast for that very reason.

Ingredients:

2.5lbs / 1Kg Neck of Lamb
1.5 lb Marrow Bone
5 Pints of water
Salt
8oz / 250g Green Peas, freshly shelled if possible
4oz / 125g Broad Beans
6 Wee Turnips, diced
6 Wee Carrots, diced
6 Spring Onions
1 Cauliflower
1 Lettuce
6 Sprigs of Parsley, finely chopped

Method:

Put the neck of Lamb and the marrow bone into the large pot with the cold water and a little salt.

Bring to the boil, and skim carefully.

Shell the peas; shell and skin the beans.

Prepare and dice the turnips and carrots

Peel and cut up the onions.

Retain half the peas, and put the rest of the prepared vegetables into the boiling liquor.

Draw to the side and simmer very gently for 3-4 hours, or longer. Ia long slow cook is best.

Meanwhile put the cauliflower and the lettuce into cold water with a little salt, and let them lie for half an hour.

Break the cauliflower into sprigs and chop the lettuce and, half an hour before serving, add them to the broth with the remainder of the peas.

Just before serving add the parsley. The soup should be nearly as thick as porridge, and is a meal in itself. Eat with crusty bread and butter!

10. Auld Reekie Steak

Auld Reekie is the affectionate name for Scotland's capital city, Edinburgh, and these steaks with the added kick of whisky is a real favourite in the pubs of the town.

Ingredients:

4 fillet steaks (about 250g each)
350ml double cream
A Splash of good whisky
120g smoked Scottish cheddar cheese
grated 25g butter
salt and freshly-ground black pepper, to taste
oil for frying

Method:

Add a little oil to a frying pan and use to pan-fry the steaks until cooked to your liking.

Remove the meat from the pan and set aside to keep warm.

Pour the whisky into the hot pan and flambé with a splint.

When the flames have died down, add the cream and the grated cheese. Stir to combine and bring gently to a simmer.

Continue to simmer gently (do not boil, or the cream may split), stirring occasionally, for about 10 minutes, or until the sauce has reduce by half.

Season to taste then beat in the butter.

Arrange the steaks on warmed plates, spoon over the sauce and serve with your choice of chips and choice of vegetables.

11. Mince and Tatties

Every little boy and girl in Scotland grew up on Mince and Tatties. This simple dish is cheap to prepare, extremely tasty and very nutritious. Enjoy this with a slice of buttered white bread on the side for a true taste of Scotland.

Ingredients:

1 tablespoon oil.
1 large onion, finely chopped.
1 lb beef mince.
2 medium carrots, sliced.
1 tablespoon toasted pinhead oatmeal.
Water to cover.
1 or 2 beef stock cubes.
Salt and pepper.
Gravy powder.
1 lb boiled potatoes, peeled.

Method:

Heat the oil in a pan and sauté the onion until it is dark brown.

Add in the mince and cook until well browned.

Add the carrots and oatmeal, mix well and pour in enough water to just cover. Crumble in the stock cubes, season and stir.

Cover the pan and simmer the mince for about 20 minutes. Once the mince is cooked thicken the mince with about 3 teaspoons of gravy powder or corn starch mixed with a little cold water.

Serve the mince boiled potatoes, green vegetables and a glass of Irn Bru.

12. Forfar Bridies

Bridies are believed to have been 'invented' in the town of Forfar in the east of Scotland. this hand held pie of sorts is similar to the Cornish Pastie without the inclusion of potatoes. The best bridies are still made in Forfar but this recipe will give them a run for their money.

Ingredients:

1½ lbs (700g) boneless, lean rump steak. Lean minced beef can also be used.
2 oz (2 rounded tablespoons) suet or butter.
1 (or 2) onion, chopped finely
1 teaspoon dry mustard powder
Quarter cup rich beef stock
Salt and pepper to taste
1½ lbs flaky pastry (home made or from a pastry mix packet)

Method:

Remove any fat or gristle from the meat and beat with a meat bat or rolling pin.

Cut into half-inch (1cm) pieces and place in a medium bowl.

Add the salt, pepper, mustard, chopped onion, suet (or butter/margarine) and stock and mix well.

Prepare the pastry and divide the pastry and meat mixture into six equal portions.

Roll each pastry portion into a circle about six inches in diameter and about quarter of an inch thick and place a portion of the mixture in the centre. Leave an edge of pastry showing all round.

Brush the outer edge of half the pastry circle with water and fold over.

Crimp the edges together well. The crimped edges should be at the top of each bridie. Make a small slit in the top (to let out any steam).

Brush a 12 inch square (or equivalent area) baking tray with oil and place the bridies in this, ensuring that they are not touching.

Place in a pre-heated oven at 450f/230c/gas mark 8 for 15 minutes then reduce the temperature to 350f/180c/gas mark 4 and cook for another 45/55 minutes. They should be golden brown and if they are getting too dark, cover with greaseproof paper.

These are delicious served hot or cold and are a wholesome addition to anyones lunch box!

13. Haggis Baws with Whisky and Mushroom Sauce

In Scotland we are constantly looking for new ways to serve haggis, our national dish, with inventive chefs creating everything from haggis pizzas to haggis ice cream. This recipe is a delicious way to serve the dish without going too far off the beaten track.

Ingredients:

For the meatballs:

1 onion
60g cream crackers for breadcrumbs
454g haggis
400g Scotch beef mince
1 egg
2 tbsp tomato puree or ketchup
salt and pepper

For the sauce:

50g mushrooms, chopped.
butter or oil
50ml whisky
250ml double cream

Method:

Preheat the oven to 180c / Gas mark 4.
Finely chop the onion and smash the cream crackers with a rolling pin in a clean tea-towel to make breadcrumbs.

Combine all ingredients into bowl, ensuring everything is mixed well along with a dash of salt and pepper.

Shape meatballs by hand into 3 to 4cm balls and set onto lightly greased oven proof dish.

Bake in the preheated oven for 20 to 30 minutes.

To make the sauce roughly chop the mushrooms into small pieces.

Add a little butter or oil to a hot pan and sauté the mushrooms for 2 to 3 minutes.

Add the whisky to the pan and then carefully burn off the alcohol by flambéing the whisky.

Add the double cream along with some salt and pepper whilst allowing the sauce to reduce.

Once the meatballs are ready; serve on plates along with the sauce and to round of the meal serve with some mashed tatties and neeps.

14. Lanarkshire Roasted Haggis

Here is another way of serving our national dish. With recipe the haggis and vegetables come together as one dish and is real comfort for cozy nights in.

Ingredients:

Serves: 4

500g baby potatoes
1 good sized turnip or swede
handful coriander seeds
2 regular sized haggis
olive oil as needed
25g butter
small handful parsley

Method:

Preheat the oven to 200c / Gas mark 6.

Leave the skins on the potatoes and put on to boil.

Peel and dice the turnip.

Crush the coriander seed in a mortar and pestle.

Wrap the haggis in tin foil.

Once the oven is hot put the haggis in the centre of the oven.

Once they are fully boiled, take the potatoes off the heat and drain. After twenty minutes put some olive oil in a roasting tray in the oven.

Once the oil is hot add the chopped turnip and crushed coriander seeds, and roast for 45 minutes.

5 minutes before the end of the cooking time, put the now cold potatoes in a pan and fry with the butter and parsley until brown and crispy on the outside.

Put the turnip into a serving dish. Slice the haggis and empty into the roasting tray used for the turnips.

Even out the haggis and garnish with a few sprigs of parsley.

15. Kedgeree

This curried fish dish might not seem traditionally Scottish, but it has been part of our diet for well over 100 years. It is thought that the idea was brought back to Scotland with soldiers returning from India in Victorian times.

Ingredients:

(To serve four people):
2 fillets of smoked haddock, bones and skin removed
2 hard boiled eggs, shelled and chopped finely
350g long grain basmati rice (or brown rice)
300ml of milk to poach the fish
50g of butter
750ml chicken stock
Small onion, peeled and finely chopped
One bay leaf
One teaspoon curry powder (or more if you are brave))
Half teaspoon grated nutmeg
Ground pepper (to taste)

Method:

Pre-heat the oven to 180c/350f/Gas Mark 4.

Cook the onion gently in the butter and add the rice, stirring to coat the rice in butter.

Add the stock and bring to the boil.

Add the bay leaf, cover and cook in the oven for about 20 minutes or until the rice has absorbed the stock.

Remove the bay leaf at the end of cooking.

Poach the fish in hot milk for five minutes and drain just before the rice is ready. Flake the fish.

When the rice is ready, stir in the flaked fish, chopped eggs, curry powder, nutmeg and pepper, using a fork to stir the flaked fish (to prevent the rice from breaking up).

Kedgeree can be served with scrambled eggs as a breakfast or with mashed tatties as a proper meal.

16. Lorne Sausage (aka Square Sausage)

A Lorne Sausage Bap (roll) is probably one of the country's favourite snack items. You can get them everywhere. they are so simple to make and so delicious that I had to include them in this book. Once you have made and sliced these up, pop them in the freezer to be brought out later, you will be glad you did when the urge for a square sausage bap come along.

Ingredients:

1lb (450 g) of fatty minced pork with no gristle
8 oz (225 g) of fatty minced beef with no gristle
1 pint of fine bread crumbs (white or wholemeal)
1 teaspoon of black pepper
1 teaspoon of allspice
Salt to taste
Approximately quarter of a pint (140 ml) of water

Method:

Mix all of the ingredients really well by hand then place in a (900 g) loaf tin.

Pop in the fridge for an hour or two until the mixture firms up.

Cut into approx half inch (1.25 cm) thick slices.

Fry until cooked through and browned on both sides.

Serve in a morning roll with brown sauce.

17. Jura Venison Collops

Here in Scotland we are extremely proud of the quality of our meat products, none more so than our Venison. It truly is the best in the world and this recipe is delicious way to do the meat justice.

Ingredients:

2 pounds (about 1 kg) of venison loin cut from the bone into 8 slices. Keep the bones and meat trimmings for the gravy.
Mixed Spices
2 oz (50 - 60 g) butter for frying meat
Further butter for thickening sauce as required
White flour
One quarter pint (150 ml) of brown gravy
One quarter pint (150 ml) of red wine
Two tablespoons (30 ml) of white wine vinegar
Two tablespoons (30 ml) of white sugar
Lemon juice squeezed from one half of a medium sized lemon
Salt to taste

Method:

Prepare the gravy by boiling up the bones and trimmings in a covered pot with water.

Strain the gravy.

Place the gravy, red wine, wine vinegar, lemon juice, sugar and salt in a pan and boil until the volume is reduced by at least one half.

Reduce the volume further depending on how intensely you wish your sauce to be flavoured.

Thicken the sauce using pieces of butter rolled in flour after it has been reduced.

Thoroughly coat the venison slices in mixed spices.

Fry the venison in butter in a very hot pan for around 5 minutes, turning once, being careful not to overcook as this tends to dry the meat.

Lower the heat and add the reduced sauce to the venison. Allow to cook for a further two minutes.

Serve with roasted potatoes and cabbage.

18. Burty's Beer Battered Fish and Chips

Scotland's favourite Friday night takeaway, Fish 'n' Chips is so simple to do at home. This recipe will serve up the freshest, most delicious meal. In Scotland there is s real east / west divide on how to season your chips. In the west, particularly the city of Glasgow, nothing goes on your chips except salt and vinager. In the east, particularly the city of Edinburgh, nothing goes on your chips apart from salt and Chippy Sauce, a kind of HP sauce with added vinegar. The choice is yours.

Ingredients:

For the fish:

50g plain flour
50g cornflour
1 tsp baking powder
turmeric
75ml lager beer
75ml sparkling water
about 1 litre sunflower oil, for frying
400g fillet sustainable cod, hake or haddock, halved

For the chips:

750g potatoes, Maris Piper or Desiree, peeled and sliced into thick chips
2 tbsp plain flour
2 tbsp sunflower oil

Method;

Combine the flour, cornflour, baking powder and turmeric in a large bowl, season, then spoon 1 tbsp onto a plate and set aside.

Gradually pour the beer and water into the bowl, stirring with a wooden spoon until you have a smooth, lump-free batter.

Leave to rest for 30 mins while you prepare the chips.

Heat oven to 200c/fan 180c/gas mark 6.

Boil a large pan of water, then add the chipped potatoes and boil for 2-3 mins until the outsides are just tender but not soft.
Drain well, then tip onto a large baking tray with the flour, oil and some salt. Gently toss together until all the potatoes are evenly coated and the flour is no longer dusty.

Roast for 30 mins, turning occasionally, until the chips are golden and crisp.

To cook the fish, heat the 1 litre oil in a deep saucepan until a drop of batter sizzles and crisps up straight away.

Pat the fish dry with kitchen paper, then toss it in the reserved turmeric flour mix. Shake off any excess, then dip into the batter.

Carefully lower each fillet into the hot oil and fry for 6-8 mins – depending on the thickness of the fish – until golden and crisp.

Using a large slotted spoon, lift out the fish, drain on kitchen paper, then sprinkle with salt and your choice of vinegar or 'Chippy' Sauce.

19. Tweed Kettle

The River Tweed is one of Scotland's longest and greatest rivers for fishing wild Salmon. This dish celebrates this great river and is now coming back in fashion. This dish deserves the best ingredients so try to use the best wild salmon you can get your hands on.

Ingredients:

2lbs fresh salmon, preferably from the tail end
2 chopped shallots or 1 tablespoon of chopped chives
Salt, pepper, pinch of ground mace
Quarter pint water
Quarter pint (150ml) dry white wine
4 Ounces chopped mushrooms
1 tablespoon chopped parsley

Method:

Put the fish in a pan, just covered with water and bring to the boil.

Simmer gently for five minutes. Remove fish from the pan (keep the stock), remove skin and bone and cut the fish into 2 inch squares.

Season with salt, pepper and mace and put into a clean dish with a quarter pint of the fish stock plus the wine and finely chopped shallot or chives.

Cover the dish and simmer gently for about 20 minutes.

Heat up the butter and soften the mushrooms in it, drain and add to the salmon and heat together for another five minutes.

Serve with chopped parsley and a good amount of clapshot.

20. Venison and Beer Cobbler

A cobbler is basically a pie of stewed meat with, instead of pastry on top, a scone type mixture is used to top the meat. This recipe, using venison instead of beef, it a hearty meal that is a warming way to satisfy your family's hunger.

Ingredients:

For The Filling:

4tbsp Olive Oil
2 Onions. finely chopped
1 Celery Stick, finely diced
1 leek, trimmed and finely sliced
150g button mushrooms, wiped halved and quatered, if needed
600 g venison stewing/casserol steak
2tbsp plain flour
sea salt and freshly ground black pepper
500 ml dark beer or porter
1 beef stock cube
1 bouquet garni
1tbsp sugar
2 large carrots, in 2cm chunks

For the Cobbler:

300 g Self raising flour, plus extra for dusting
1tsp baking powder
1/2 tsp salt
125g unsalted butter, chilled and diced
1tsp finely chopped parsley
3tbsp horseraddish sauce or horse raddish cream
2-4 tbsp milk
1 egg, beaten for glazing

Method:

In large ovenproof casserole dish, heat 2 tablespoons olive oil and fry the onion, celery and leek for about 5 mins, until soft but not brown.

Add the mushrooms and fry for 2-3 minutes until they begin to colour in places.

Remove the vegetables with a slotted spoon and set aside.

Toss the venison in 2 table spoons seasoned flour.

Heat the remaining oil in the casserole and fry the meat, a few pieces at a time, until

well browned on all sides.
Remove the meat as it cooks and add it to the vegetables.

Return the meat to the casserole with the vegetables, and cover with the beer.

Crumble over the stock cube and add 300 ml boiling water, bouquet garni, sugar and carrots.

Check for seasoning, and bring to a boil.

Reduce the heat to its lowest setting, cover, and cook for 1 – 1 ½ hours until the meat is tender.
Check it from time to time and top up the water if needed.

Preheat the oven to 200c.

Sift together the flour, baking powder and salt.

Using your finger tips rub in the butter until the mixture resembles bread crumbs.

Add the parsley. Whisk the horseradish sauce and milk, and use the liquid to bind the dry ingredients to form a soft dough.

On a floured surface, roll out the dough to a thickness of 2 cm. Using a pastry cutter cut out circles.

When the stew is cooked remove the Bouquet Garni and top it with the disks if the cobbler dough.

Overlap them slightly so that there are very few gaps where the filling can be seen.

Brush the tops with the beaten egg, and bake the cobbler for 30-40 mins until it is puffed up and golden brown.

Remove it from the oven and let rest for 5 mins before serving.

21. Balmoral Chicken

Named after the Queens Highland estateBalmoral Chicken is a classic dish seen up and down the country on Gastro Pub and Restaurant menus. Sometimes the dish is smothered in a cream whisky sauce but I prefer it this way with the crispy bacon and the punch of whisky coming from the haggis.

Ingredients:

Serves: 4

4 to 6 tablespoons whisky
250g haggis
salt and pepper, to taste
4 skinless chicken breasts
16 rashers smoked streaky bacon

Method:

Preheat the oven to 160c / Gas mark 3. Grease an oven proof baking dish.

In a bowl, mix together the whisky and the haggis. Season well. Divide into four and form each into a sausage shape. Set aside.

Butterfly the chicken breasts and beat them to flatten. They should flatten to about the same length as the bacon rashers.

Lay 4 rashers of bacon neatly with some slight overlap out on a sheet of cling film. Lay one flattened chicken breast out on top of the 4 rashers of bacon.

Place a haggis 'sausage' at the edge of the breast. Carefully roll up to form a parcel using the cling film to help you. Take care to keep the haggis hidden and the bacon neat.

Once rolled into a tight parcel, secure with kitchen string and remove from the cling film and arrange inside the prepared baking dish. Cover with tin foil. Repeat a further three times.

Bake in the preheated oven for 25 minutes, removing the tin foil for an additional 8 minutes.

Once the bacon is nicely browned, remove from the oven and allow to rest for a few minutes.

Serve hot with boiled tatties and vegetables of your choice.

22. Cabbie Claw

Cabbie Claw, is a well known recipe from the north-east of Scotland and the Orkney Isles for a dish of cod fillets in an egg sauce. Originally salted cod was used, but today it's much more common to use fresh cod fillets. This dish was first introduced to me in hotel in Lerwick on Orkney where the chef had written on the menu "If I were a cod I'd give my life to become this dish".

Ingredients :

1 lb (450 g) fillet of cod
1 tsp horseradish root, grated
1 tbsp parsley, chopped
salt and pepper to taste
2 tbsp (1 oz) 25 g butter
1 lb (450 g) hot potatoes, mashed
a little milk
2 tbsp (1 oz) 25 g butter
3 tbsp (25 g) self raising (self rising) flour
1 1/4 cups (10 fl oz) 300 ml milk
1 medium hard boiled egg
cayenne pepper

Method:
For the Fish:

Put the fish in a saucepan with the horseradish, parsley, salt and pepper and sufficient water to cover.

Bring to the boil, then simmer for about 15 minutes until the fish is cooked.

Lift out the fish, retain the liquid, remove the skin and bones and flake roughly.

Put on to a hot, shallow dish and keep warm.

In the meantime, beat the butter into the mashed potato with sufficient milk to give a creamy consistency.

Fork the potato mixture round the fish, or pipe a border, and keep warm.

For the Sauce:

Melt the butter, stir in the flour and gradually add the milk to 150 ml (5 fl oz) of the strained fish liquid.

Bring to the boil and cook for 3 minutes.

Chop the hard boiled egg white and stir into the sauce with salt and pepper to taste.
Gently pour the sauce over the fish.
Sieve the egg yolk and sprinkle, together with the cayenne pepper, over the top of the sauce.

23. Roast Rack of Lamb with Herb Crust

Ingredients:

(for six people):
2 oz/56g butter
2 tbsp olive oil
1 onion, finely chopped
1 clove of garlic, finely chopped
6 oz/170 g 1 day old breadcrumbs
Salt and pepper
2 tbsp each of finely chopped parsley, chives and tarragon
2 racks of lamb each with 6 - 7 chops in it

Method:

Melt the butter and heat the oil together and sauté the onion in this till it is really soft - about 5 minutes.

Stir in the garlic and cook for a minute. Then stir in the breadcrumbs, salt and pepper and take off the heat.

Add the mixed herbs and mix thoroughly
T
rim all the fat you can from the racks lay them so that the fat is facing up.

Spoon over the herb crust, pressing it down well, and roast in a hot oven, 400f /200c/ Gas mark 6, for 25 - 30 minutes.

Slice and serve with clapshot or mashed tatties and green vegetables.

24. Cranachan

Apart from haggis I don't think there is any dish more Scottish than Cranachan. This luscious desert full of cream, raspberries, whisky, oatmeal and honey is a blend of Scotland's finest natural ingredients that should be an advert for the country. Make this once and it will you dinner part finale for years to come.

Ingredients:

1lb/500g raspberries
6 tbsp whisky
3oz/75g pinhead oatmeal
3 tbsp Heather Honey
1pt/600 ml Double cream

Method:

Spread oatmeal on a baking sheet and toast in a medium oven until crisp for 3-6 minutes.

Leave cool.

Whip the cream until it is thick but not stiff.

Blend all the raspberries (except 2 which are for decoration) until they form a smooth purée.

Combine oatmeal, whisky, honey and cream and raspberries.

Spoon the mixture into tall glasses

Chill for an hour or two before serving.

Just before serving, decorated if you wish with freshly whipped cream, a few fresh raspberries and drizzled with a wee bit honey.

25. Shortbread

Although not a Scottish 'dish' as such, no Scottish cookbook could be without shortbread. The little butter, sweet biscuits are served up with tea and coffee throughout the land as a little treat. Be warned!!! One is never enough!

Ingredients:

1lb (500g)plain flour
1lb (500g) self raising flour
1lb (500g) butter
8oz (225g) castor sugar
Half teaspoon salt

Method:

Cream the butter and sugar together.

Combine with the sieved flour and salt. Use finger tips and do this gently.

Shape into 2 rounds with your hands.

Put on a baking tray.

Pinch the edges with your finger and thumb to give a nice finish.

Prick the base all over with a fork.

Bake in a low oven, 140c/ 275f / Gas 1 for around 1 hour.

Leave to cool, cut into the required shape.

Turn onto a rack.

26. Scottish Butter Tablet

For everyone with a sweet toot there is nothing better than a wee bite of Scottish Tablet. This sweety is sometime compared to the better known dairy fudge, but Scottish tablet is more crumbly, sugar affair. Make this recipe and enjoy the naughtier side of life.

Ingredients:

2lbs (1 kg) Granulated Sugar
4 oz (113g) Unsalted Butter
One 14oz (396g) can of Condensed Milk
8 fl. oz (227ml) of Milk
1 fl. oz (3 dssp) Natural Vanilla Essence

Method:

Lightly grease a baking tray (11 x 19 inches works well) with butter and set aside.

Put the sugar and milk into a fairly large, heavy stainless steel saucepan (mixture will double in quantity as it heats).

Stir together. Add the butter and condensed milk and stir again.

Put the pan on a medium-high heat and bring mixture to the boil, stirring occasionally.

Once mixture comes to the boil, reduce the heat until mixture is boiling gently.

Continue to let it boil for around 20 - 30 minutes, still stirring occasionally.

Remove saucepan from the heat and add Vanilla Essence

Beat the mixture vigorously for 4 - 5 minutes, or until the mixture starts to feel more 'stiff' and 'gritty' under the spoon.

At this point the Tablet is ready to be poured into the baking tray you prepared at the beginning.

Allow mixture to cool a little and then mark it off into bars, or squares with a sharp knife.

Tablet is ready to eat when fully cooled.

27. Sláinte

Thank you so much again for reading my book and I sincerely hope you have enjoyed trying out these recipes. If you live in Scotland I hope these recipes have rekindled you love of Scottish food and If you are from further afield I hope to welcome you to Scotland one day and spoil you with our generosity.

- Sláinte
Margaret Mochrie

Printed in Great Britain
by Amazon.co.uk, Ltd.,
Marston Gate.